THE POWER
OF SYMBOLS

Sacred Images for Meditation, Divination, and Coloring

THE POWER
Sacred Images for Meditation, Divination, and Coloring
OF SYMBOLS

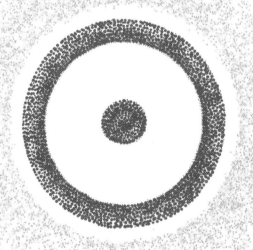

Stefano Fusi

BEYOND WORDS
Portland, Oregon

1750 S.W. Skyline Blvd., Suite 20
Portland, Oregon 97221-2543
503-531-8700 / 503-531-8773 fax
www.beyondword.com

This first Beyond Words paperback edition June 2025
Previously published by Edizioni LAlbero in 2021, ISBN: 9788897551621

Copyright © 2021 by Stefano Fusi

All rights reserved, including the right to reproduce this book or portions thereof in any form.

BEYOND WORDS PUBLISHING and colophon are registered trademarks of Beyond Words Publishing. Beyond Words is an imprint of Simon & Schuster, LLC.

For more information about special discounts for bulk purchases, please contact Beyond Words Special Sales at 503-531-8700 or specialsales@beyondword.com.

Managing editor: Lindsay Easterbrooks-Brown
Editors: Michele Ashtiani Cohn, Bailey Potter
Proofreader: Ashley Van Winkle
Illustrations: Stefano Fusi
Cover Design: Cristina Arianna Oliva, Sara E. Blum
Design: Sara E. Blum

Manufactured in the China

10 9 8 7 6 5 4 3 2 1

The corporate mission of Beyond Words Publishing, Inc.: *Inspire to Integrity*

To Lorenzo Ostuni

What are symbols?
The highest energy in the lowest form.

Lorenzo Ostuni, from "Love Heals Life"

CONTENTS

Introduction: Traces of Infinity 1

Part 1: Exploring the Shapes of the Soul 7
    What Is a Symbol? 12
    Sacred Symbols 16
    Exploring Sacred Symbols 20
    How to Use This Book and the Illustrations 22
    Visualization and Meditation on the Symbol 27
    Reproducing the Symbols 28
    Recording Messages, Evoking, and Representing the Symbol 31

Part 2: Sacred Symbols 33
    1: Kapemni—The Mirror of the Universe on Earth 36
    2: Totem Pole—The Great Living Family 37
    3: Tzolk'in and Haab—The Maya Calendar 38
    4: Chakana—The Andean Cross 39
    5: Mata Komoe—The Sign of Value 40
    6: Tjurunga—The Dreamtime Map 41
    7: Ensō—The Zen Circle 42
    8: Torii—The Sacred Portal 43
    9: Bagua—The Flow of Energies 44
    10: Dorje—The Purity of Mind 45
    11: Dharmachakra—The Wheel of the Law 46
    12: Om—The Creative Vibration 47
    13: Lingam-Yoni—The Cosmic Union 48
    14: Faravahar—The Pact with Goodwill 49
    15: Māgēn Dāwīd—The Seal of Solomon 50
    16: Etz Hayim—The Tree of Life 51

17: Cross—The Meeting in the Heart 52

18: Ichthýs—The Fish of Christ 53

19: Crescent Moon—The Light of the Soul 54

20: Khamsa—The Hand of Fatima 55

21: Ankh—The Key to Eternal Life 56

22: Udjat—The Eye of Horus 57

23: Mask—The True Face 58

24: Nyame Ye Ohene—Divine Sovereignty 59

25: Labyrinth—The Inner Journey 60

26: Labrys—The Bipennis Axe 61

27: Caduceus—The Divine Messenger 62

28: The Goddess—The Divine Feminine 63

29: Camunian Rose—The Memory of the World 64

30: Etruscan Liver and Mirror—The Oracular Signs 65

31: Ouroboros and the Alchemical Pot—Transmutation through
Time and Space 66

32: Vitruvian Man—At the Center of the World 67

33: Triskele—The Triple Spiral 68

34: Valknut and the Runes—The Search for Divine Knowledge 69

35: Vegvísir—The Spiritual Compass 70

36: Beaivi—The Sun Drum of the Sámi 71

37: Kolovrat—The Radiating Sun 72

38: Sword—The Weapon of Virtue 73

39: Spiral—The Primary Motion 74

40: Infinity—Union with the Whole 75

41: Dot and Circle—The Symbol of Symbols 76

Part 3: Sacred Symbols for Coloring, Meditation, and Divination 77

Author's Note 163

Acknowledgments 165

About the Author 167

INTRODUCTION
Traces of Infinity

Many years ago I was following meditation practices and techniques based on visualization, which allows access to wide mental spaces. I had been painting for some time—I have always done it, ever since I could hold a pencil, a brush, or a marker. As I painted, meaningful images emerged. Over time I came to understand that these images were messages.

I was exploring, as I still do in art, life, work, and inner research. Through meditation, a living image came to me—a symbol that spoke, a spiritual ally, who introduced himself then as Athanor. He was a man-falcon and looked like an actual friend of mine whom I knew to be a medium, but at the same time, Athanor seemed to be made of sky and stars. He was wrapped in a cloak that made him visible and tangible, so to speak, with a half-human and half-bird face—both at the same time, as wave and particle. Only later did I discover the alchemical meaning of his name: Athanor is the crucible where transmutations take place, the furnace in which we are digested and reshaped, melted, and coagulated in the alchemical work—transformed into new forms. He suggested a path that I obviously struggled to understand and follow immediately, and that I still try to understand and follow.

I don't feel special because of this message I received: we can all access this inner space and get help and guidance from our spiritual core.

Each of us has within, behind, and beside us entities that are simply our essence in the parallel world of spirit—the parallel world in which we always reside, even at this very moment, and which we are only able to perceive at times. Just as each person has beside them those who are yet unborn, those with whom they live this earthly experience, and those who have died on this physical world but are still, always, alive.

Athanor was a person, but he was at the same time a universal entity: he represented the infinity that is in me, in each of us. He also represented something else, which I still don't know of and maybe I will never find out. It also appeared in the form of a symbol, that of the five-pointed star, and the five points were themselves stars. Each star had a name: Loyalty, Love, Effort, Loneliness, Happiness. Athanor told me that when I came to follow these stars well, I would be happy with myself and in life. He explained them to me, not verbally but with the equivalent of a voice in that subtle telepathic communication we had. He told me that the stars are all symbolic and that together they make up the sacred pentacle of the human being.

- **Loyalty:** An inner loyalty to things that deserve respect and deference; a commitment to life.

- **Love:** A love for life, for what is close to me.

- **Effort:** A perseverance in the face of difficulties; to not give up; to strive; to have conviction and make my best effort; to overcome pain by learning from challenges.

- **Loneliness:** An acceptance of loneliness, and understanding it as necessary for me to get to where I want to go. And I must hold on and not give in to defeat or loss, even if the people around me don't understand. This applies to others as well, as a mirror: we often can't understand others, but others are ourselves in other forms.

- **Happiness:** The use of my energy; transforming it, regenerating it continuously, giving thanks to it; smiling; giving.

This symbolic vision accompanied me for years. Later, others came, each one important and appropriate to the situation I was going through at the time—the source of these symbolic images is as inexhaustible as life and brings valuable signals and indications in every period and event of life.

In the last few years, as in the early years of my experiences as well, I get mostly spirals. The symbols have me always spiraling on the underlying themes of the soul, on the same issues—either spiraling across wider areas or coming back to the original ones—and when my age advanced, the spiral changed direction.

Years after that event, the symbols that appeared to me and that I painted inspired me to write this work.

Nature is the great artist.
Her beauty is divine love.
Art is adoration.
With gratitude I receive and transmit the emotions, shapes, and
  colors of the forces that animate the living world and inner life.
To express oneself is to continue the work of nature.
To paint and draw is to trace the spirit on earth.
To illustrate is to conceive the children of stories and tales.
To decorate nature is to honor the sacred.
To share art is to celebrate the community of all living things.

I finally realized why I drew, painted, and did everything I did and do—because I am nature and spirit myself, as we all are. Art is not only aesthetic; it is also a vehicle for meaning.

Then I began to explore the symbols themselves, beyond the countless forms in which they disguise themselves. I arrived at the nucleus. For this discovery I am indebted to masters who opened my mind, heart, and way; among them was Lorenzo Ostuni, Italian alchemist of the soul, artist, and haruspex who reinvigorated and continued the tradition of the ancient sibyls and oracles, transferring their wisdom to the modern world so it may quench its thirst at the Source. With him I experienced the symbols of his magical mirrors, oracular ways, and biodrama. In one extraordinary experience not unlike a baptism of sorts, I returned to life from the water, accompanied by loving hands and hearts and bodies until I found myself in front of the mirror where I saw myself for the first time, together with others, and it was a great joy shared with so many explorers of the soul.

Something I have learned, among the infinity of things that often stay hidden, is that beyond what we perceive with our senses is a vast world without boundaries. Beyond what we call matter is an immense field of which we are a very small part: it is what we call the divine, the Spirit. Beyond the manifest, there is the unmanifest, what we cannot see or feel directly. Beyond the earth on which we walk and where our body dwells, there is the heaven in which we move and where our mind reaches. We can grasp, at times, only glimmers of this vast world that is beyond our common experience; we can conceive it and have a vague idea of it but not experience it completely. Symbols help us to experience it and re-establish a relationship within us between body, soul, and spirit; between concrete and abstract; rational and intuitive; visible and invisible. This is done through the imagination and intuition.

Symbols are the signs that reveal and perpetuate the unlimited universe in our world and common life. They reveal meanings beyond those obvious to the senses and to our rational sphere. They exist before we can imagine or think about them. Like genes and DNA on the physical plane, symbols pre-exist us—they carry with them the original instructions of life. They exist in nature, and our ancestors encoded them to express the essential forces that have structured existence since the very beginning of time in perceptible and comprehensible forms. They are a synthetic map of the motions of what we call energy, the energy that emerges from the void and permeates it, bringing to light everything that exists in this incredible adventure that we live every moment.

Symbols tell us who we are, where we come from, where we are going, how we transform and evolve, and even of the powers that animate, rule, and govern the cosmos. They cure and heal us from the wounds and illusions caused by separation and grief. They make us feel part of a whole, part of the great universal family.

Sacred symbols are artistic expressions of spiritual and religious beliefs and forms. They speak directly to our psychic sphere, immediately revealing to the soul concepts that our analytical mind cannot grasp, since the latter has the task of subdividing the whole into parts to understand them on the level of daily life.

Symbols are pure light transmuted into images. They are keys to approach the vast field of the Spirit, to reach the creative Source. This Source speaks, and its language is mysterious and very clear at the same time. Mysterious because it is beyond our common experience, and very clear for the same reason. That is, it comes directly from the collective unconscious and superconscious to our individual subconsciouses.

The language of symbols is understood by the body and the soul more than by the rational mind. The latter, not always a faithful servant, does not need symbols to function but signs. On this physical, 3D world, symbols are read as signs or glyphs. A plus sign (+), for example, is a mathematical symbol or a road sign, not a religious cross; a line (—) is a directional marker and not an indication of an inner event. The signs tells us how to function and the symbols, how to live.

Our soul and heart—where the true foundation of our life resides: intuition, love, dreams, movement, communication—need symbols. For many ancient and non-Western cultures, it is not the brain but the heart that is the seat of knowledge and inner vision. In this space, glyphs become sacred, like hieroglyphics. Like one of the most ancient crosses, the Egyptian crux ansata (or Ankh) symbol acts as a key that opens the door to eternal life.

Symbols are solid light, love in action: union, meaning, wholeness, and beauty.

Working with and meditating on sacred symbols don't just create a path to personal growth. They are acts of mental and spiritual rebirth, an intervention of collective cleansing. It is a great help in this historical period in which we are dominated by images of all kinds that flatten us on an external perception, filling us with toxins and pollution. The over-abundance of signs, icons, messages, visual stimuli of all kinds depletes the soul and crushes our imaginative capacities. The inability to concentrate and reflect, exacerbated by continuous online immersion and instant messaging, is a serious obstacle to the original expansion of free and conscious thoughts and clear intentions in life. Imagination is the force that shapes our lives: if we become dependent on external images, we are no longer able to access the inner ones. By getting back in touch with the ancient symbols, which are sacred and full of meaning, we can break out of the illusions and reconnect with the source of awareness.

In this unique book, and *The Power of Symbols Deck*, I propose to connect with the energy of symbols to receive and use their power. Their power is to shape reality: they are eternal and universal molds that give meaning to our lives. In these forty-one illustrations, I present forty sacred symbols (plus one more: the ineffable "symbol of symbols," from which the rest all derive) and the inspiration they have given me, both in graphic and written form. The illustrations are more complete and direct in expressing their sacred messages than the written descriptions of the symbols, but I wanted to keep these written summaries short. Contrary to what often happens in books where the images are created after the text is written, the opposite happens in *The Power of Symbols* and *The Power of Symbols Deck*—the images were born first. After all, in our human history, images are born first and then words. Even we ourselves are images.

Part 1

Exploring the Shapes of the Soul

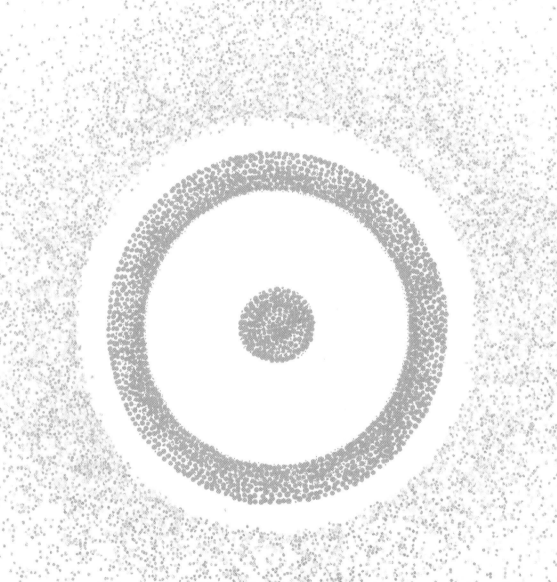

The soul is the bridge between body and spirit. It expresses itself in the form of images and sounds—images invisible to the eyes but just as real as anything we can see. The imaginal sphere is the psychic space that connects the unconscious to the conscious, the visible to the invisible, the immeasurable to the comprehensible. Here, the creative energy of nature expresses the fundamental forces of life and the world, what we call the *divine*. This divine nature is not immediately accessible to our limited human experience. The Whole that includes everything in itself is more than the sum of its parts. It is an organic and immense whole to which we have given various names, but which remains a mystery.

In this respect, when I use the term *divine*, I am not referring to a personal god or goddess, an object of faith, or the deity of a specific religion; I mean the omnipresent sacredness of the world, which can be seen in different ways according to one's tradition, consciousness, and knowledge. I do not use the term lightly because I know it can be misunderstood, for example, by those who follow an organized religion as well as by those who do not believe in any form of spirituality. But there isn't a more appropriate term to indicate what the symbols are vehicles of.

Carl Jung often used the word *numinous* to describe a state of amazement (or even awe) for the sacred and supernatural. In this book, the appearance of symbols is a numinous event. The truths they reveal are dazzling.

Yet words are limited, if necessary, tools while images are more immediate and free. But both are forms of expression that are needed to communicate. I have drawn the symbols freely, having been inspired by them in my study and need to *live* them. I have also attempted to put into words what I have gleaned from their depictions, speaking to our rational and analytical sides, which we need as much as the other, more intuitive side. After all, we need both legs to walk well, both wings to fly. You may choose to skip reading the descriptions in favor of meditating on the symbols and even coloring the images, or you may want to read the descriptions before meditating on and coloring them, because the rational sphere is also important. Both approaches are appropriate.

The symbolic images that emerge within the psyche are as real as those we see with our eyes open. It's important, though, to acknowledge that it is not us who perceive or create the mental images—we *are* images. We live *on* images and *are* images just as we live on and are earth, food, air, water, and fire.

The soul of each of us is given a unique daimon before we are born, and it has selected an image or pattern that we live on earth. This soul-companion, the daimon, guides us here; in the process of arrival, however, we forget all that took place and believe we come empty into this world. The daimon remembers what is in your image and belongs to your pattern, and therefore your daimon is the carrier of your destiny.
—James Hillman

Through symbols we gain access to the imaginal world, while verbal language allows only a small amount. The intrinsic nature of the universe on the human plane is expressed in symbols, which become myths, stories, images, celebrations, dreams, visions, art, and science. If we learn to read them, we can find them everywhere, every day.

The very structure of reality is an immense image. The world simply exists, but at the same time, it is shaped by our perceptions, it is how we see and understand it thanks to our sensory faculties and emotional, spiritual, mental, and physical perceptions. Proof of this can be seen in how there are different views of the world, both on a personal and collective level, according to places, times, and specific conditions. We see only a part of the vast reality just as we can only perceive certain frequencies of sounds and colors—the entire spectrum is closed to us even though we know it exists and other living creatures are able to tap into it. In the limited world of the senses, however, we can catch a glimpse of the whole through symbols, which act as a bridge to the invisible.

What Is a Symbol?

The term *symbol* comes from the ancient Greek word σύμβολον (*súmbo-lon*, "sign"). In turn, this derives from the verb *symballo*, whose roots are *sym*, "together," and *bàllein*, "to throw," that is "to put together," to unite two (or more) parts of a whole that had been divided. In ancient Greece, a tile, tablet, or coin (originally stone) was often divided in two so that two people who made a pact with one another each kept one half as a sign of friendship and alliance. The possibility of reuniting them and making them match testified to the existence of the alliance and allowed them to recognize the other member of the pact even if much time had passed. Well, the concept of the sacred symbol is precisely the sign of our pact with the world, with the other half of our being: the spiritual one. It allows us to recognize ourselves as part of a larger whole; it binds the sensitive to the supersensitive; it acts as a bridge between us and the cosmos.

The opposite of symbol in Greek is *diabolo*, or "devil," from the word *dia-bàllein*, which means to separate, to put an obstacle, or to divide (and slander). *Symbol* therefore stands for union, love, and truth, and the opposite meanings of the word are disunity, hatred, falsehood, and lies.

In fact, everything is a symbol. Our mind works through symbols, not only thanks to perceptions; it reflects and imagines even in their absence, starting from things that are not present to the senses. This is the special gift we have been given, just as other animals have been given the gift of flying or breathing in water: we humans can create codes and languages that, when shared, shape the world we live in. In art, science, and every sphere of our lives, we operate through symbols to which we attribute a conventional meaning and that we decode so we may better understand, operate, and live in the world around us. Sounds, signs, words, movements, expressions—everything is real and at the same time symbolic.

The human being is itself a symbol. Like the body, every natural element, living being, and artificial object can also be interpreted symbolically.

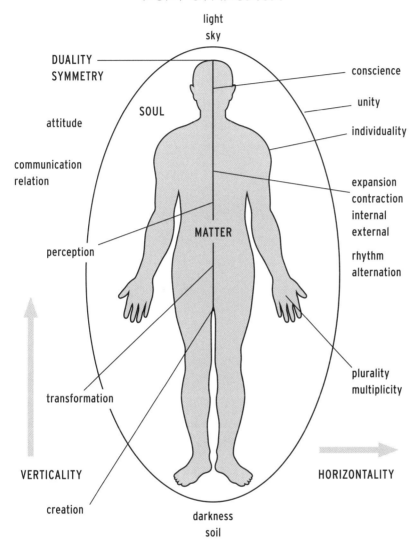

The human body, for example, is a symbol of many things:

- Unity—it is one

- Duality—it has dual parts

- Symmetry—such as right and left

- Multiplicity—fingers and toes, for example

- Union—arises from two different bodies coming together

- Creativity—produces other bodies in the union; produces things, relationships

- Consciousness—senses

- Matter—it is solid

- Animation—it moves

- Spirit—it breathes

- Ascension and verticality

- Descension and horizontality

- Motion

- Stasis

- And so on to infinity

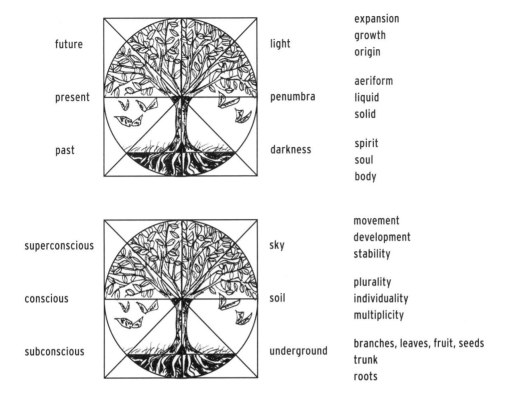

A symbol can be a gesture, an action, a graphic sign, a sound, and anything that refers to another thing or concept by indicating its direction and showing it to our minds, even if it is not physically present. In fact, in modern language, the term *symbol* designates an image that represents something else, but in this case we reduce it to an indicator sign (road signs, emoticons, trademarks, and logos) or a metaphor (the eagle: a symbol of power; the sky: a symbol of the spirit). The term *icon* (used to denote sacred images of Byzantine and Orthodox traditions, for example) is now used to define both the images on the screen of a computer or smartphone with which we indicate a type of file, app, or program, as well as a well-known character from a movie TV show, sports, or books who becomes a "symbol" of an era or a genre.

But there is an even more powerful category of symbols: sacred ones.

Sacred Symbols

A sacred symbol is part of a special class of signs. It does not merely refer to something that is not present and visible; it is not merely the depiction of an abstract concept or thought. It is that, too, but it represents a concrete psychic reality in itself, with intrinsic value.

Some symbols have existed for centuries or millennia. Therefore, they are charged with the energy of millennia of meditation and prayer, and in turn promote meditation and prayer.

Besides being ceremonial and meditation tools, they can also be divination tools. Divining is not reading the future as the fortune teller does, listening to one's own illusions, or following one's own fears and desires. It is preparing for the future by listening to the divine while full of hope. Divining is not an action, or rather, it is not a human action—the human being is only its intermediary.

As all words are transcribed in letters (or ideograms), so all images are formed by essential signs that become symbols. Some motifs of spiritual symbols are universal, common in every age and in every part of the world. Likewise, their function as a vehicle of otherworldly content is common to all cultural areas, traditions, and eras.

Like DNA strands, symbols are original coded instructions that we reproduce simply by living. Their origin is the same as that of natural forces: they arise from the motions of energy organized in fields, structures, and forms. Our imaginative mind can recognize them in the simplest visual signs, and later, we elaborate them in more articulated graphic depictions. Just as the footprints of an animal on the ground tell us that a certain species has passed there, so do the symbols reveal to us the signs of the passage of the divine in the world. Thanks to them, we can know where it comes from and in which direction it goes and leads us.

There are some basic shapes from which symbols take origin and lifeblood: they are the seeds of meaning from which the symbol germinates and grows.

- Point • unity, uniqueness, origin, center

- Line — direction, development, extension

- Cross ✛ meeting between human and divine, between verticality and horizontality

- Circle ○ circularity, perfection, harmony

- Infinity ∞ the double circle, infinite, totality

- Square ☐ balance, completeness, symmetry

- Triangle △ elevation, order, definition

- Spiral ☉ time, development, growth, evolution and involution, rhythm

The original symbol is a point surrounded by a circle: the origin, before the directional development (symbolized by the line, also that of the spiral).

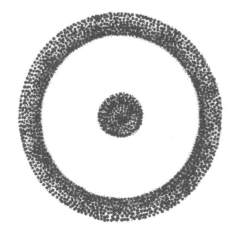

The sacred and spiritual symbols we examine in this book have been assigned a specific meaning over time and have become signs of recognition and identity of religious movements or beliefs that are not hierarchically organized but are widespread in communities. Yet each has universal value.

By studying the symbols and comparing them, one discovers in fact that some basic themes are common to all:

- The union between heaven and earth, between high and low, between human and divine

- The correspondence between cosmos and microcosm

- The complementariness and interweaving of opposites

- Unity beyond divisions

- The Three in One; the unity that manifests itself in three forms

- The quaternary: the four directions of space that meet in the circle

- The threshold of the sacred; the gateway to the divine space

- The search for oneself and one's reflection in the world

- The oneness of the universal principle

- And at the same time, the plurality of its manifestations

By observing and comparing the symbols, by meditating on them, one grasps both the original unity of the world and the phantasmagorical plurality of its manifestations. Nature is the manifested body of the divine;

therefore it, too, is infinite and multiform even though in every time and place it has similar manifestations in its environments. Comparing the sacred symbols, therefore—which are the visual manifestation of a light shown in the world in the form of spiritual consciousness—we arrive at the common core of all spiritual paths.

Today we can learn about all the symbols and traditions thanks to cultural exchange, online access to information, more frequent communication, and religious freedom, and we can no longer ignore this fact: that there are infinite ways to the absolute or, rather, that we can recognize the divinity in the sense of the All that includes the entire universe, and that none of these symbols is the only truth—they are all true and valid, although they come from different conditions and points of view. Just as today we can fly and go into space, seeing the earth physically from above and even as a whole, something that until a century ago was thought to be impossible to us, thus recognizing it as one, united, and unique. So, now we can see what unites and goes beyond the distinctions of individual faiths, and from above see how all those rivers flow toward the same oceans and come from the same sky.

This vision helps us to realize that peace and sharing, respect, and the evolution of consciousness go hand in hand with the appearance of what was once invisible. It makes us aware of the unity of all things, of the subtle mechanisms and wonderful realities of the fundamental forces that hold together, form, and shape the entire universe. Knowing that this harmony exists is like going beyond death, it is knowing that the world is all a manifestation of light that becomes image, substance, flesh, experience, and love.

This book is meant invite you to welcome and nourish these seeds of consciousness and enjoy their sweet fruits. Their fibers, vitamins, and juices transform us and give us health.

Exploring Sacred Symbols

A symbol without love, without goodwill, *or to put it in more sociological terms,* without participation, *is not a symbol. If when I touch the symbol I do not touch myself, it is not a symbol. Only when we are and are not in it does the symbol exist as such, because there is still something else. . . . When we think about the symbol it vanishes, and as soon as we attempt to understand what the symbol means, it begins to dissolve.*
—Raimon Panikkar

Symbols can be used consciously to shape our lives. They awaken unconscious contents that were dormant. The inner stories and images that arise from visualizing the symbol are important data about us. The ideas and insights that flow from them are powerful guides, to be recorded immediately on paper, or otherwise, to be remembered in detail.

Who and what does the symbol work for? It is useful for those who . . .

- are going through a period of transformation and need to find direction in their lives.

- are going through a difficult period of crisis, so they may draw on models and strong spiritual references of great support and existential direction.

- are trying to reach a synthesis of divergent thoughts and reflections.

- work in education, communication, or the helping professions because it allows them to use an imaginative tool with great evocative power and very relevant practical effects: the symbol is a catalyst for unconscious processes and a tool to activate the potential for growth and self-healing, to convey emotional content within their communication to the outside world, to share their vision, to clarify and communicate their goals, to find alliances, and to pursue their goals in the professional field.

- work in psychology, psychoanalysis, or therapeutic professions (counselors, coaches) because of the potential value of using the symbols in the illustrations in a projective test. By reading and decoding the symbols, the user allows access in a simple and effective way to the subconscious mind, so it could be interesting to conduct a project based on the data and information collected from such a test.

- enjoy mind-body expression, therapies, and disciplines for wellness; art therapy; or meditation, because it integrates the experiential journey with an in-depth reflection on the sources, origins, and assumptions and potential of these disciplines and avenues of research.

- love artistic expression or are professionally involved in graphics and illustration, painting and figurative arts, tattooing, jewelry, or artistic crafts because it represents a source of inspiration and stimulates creativity.

- are scholars and lovers of spirituality, religions, and esotericism, because it goes to the root of the traditions examined and reveals their essence through one of the most direct ways—that of the imaginary sphere.

How to Use This Book and the Illustrations

One can also use this book only for the pleasure of getting to know the symbols, out of intellectual curiosity. In working with the illustrations, they still act on our unconscious, giving us their unique qualities. But you can do more: use the images to deepen, to discover, and to use their healing energy. All symbols are valid, powerful, and safe aids, activating mental and spiritual energies. Studying them, visualizing them, examining their meanings is already a way to work on oneself: their powers act immediately, even if you simply dwell on their image and meaning.

Each of the sacred symbols emphasizes some aspect of existence, and therefore, inevitably, one of them cannot correspond completely to your entire personality. Nevertheless, it highlights some aspects of it, in relation to whatever current situation is in your mind.

You may already have a favorite symbol or one that you feel closest to, or you may encounter one here that represents an integration of meaning in the transition you are experiencing in this precise moment. However,

it would be useful to accept whichever sacred symbol best corresponds to you in this moment: the one you need, the one that can lead you to an important turning point. You may also feel close to more than one symbol, in which case, it'd be good to work with two or three of them at once.

The first and most powerful way to use this book is as a divination tool. This greatly helps the subsequent work of interpreting, processing, representing, and physically realizing the symbol itself. To divine is to make oneself available for transformation, to be humble, and to accept the fact that life—the universal mind that understands us (and takes us in)—knows much more than our limited individual minds. To divine is to open oneself to the mystery. It does not mean to abdicate one's sovereignty; on the contrary, it is a way to loosen the excessive control we exert over ourselves even when it is not needed. It is to trust in life, to harmonize with its processes, which are not elementary mechanisms in the mold of artificial systems to which we are accustomed and conformed, but complex, multiform, surprising energy flows. The unpredictable, the numinous, and the exception to the rule are realities, too, even if they cannot be programmed or framed. And precisely for this reason, they are more significant than routine. In order to recognize the sacred in ourselves, we need to be open to the poetry of the moment. In order to live better, we also need to dream, to fantasize, to abandon ourselves to the support of the vastness and wisdom of life—just as in order to float, we need to let ourselves go with confidence. The water of the sea sustains us even if we do not swim. We don't always risk drowning if we let go. Trying to swim is useful in emergencies or very volatile situations, but when the sea water is calm, we can do without it. In any case, there is also a way to open up to randomness without fear or skepticism: it is *ordered randomness*, or the integration between abandonment and control, as Alan Watts, one of the greatest scholars of Zen and Eastern ways of knowledge, explained.

Relying on the present moment and on the synchronic wisdom of life is the first step in the direction of meditation and spiritual opening. You can choose one or more symbols by selecting from the illustrations at random. This can be done in either of two ways:

- flipping through parts 2 and 3 of the book and choosing a page at random, by instinct and intuition, relying on natural attraction

- consciously scanning parts 2 and 3 and choosing (by intuition or aesthetic suggestion) the symbol and image that inspires, attracts, or intrigues you

Even pure curiosity is never really curiosity—we usually define that term as the attraction to mystery and the need to discover something about oneself that goes beyond everyday experience. It is a mask of our true needs, well layered and concealed by habits.

However, I recommend divining with imagery only after clarifying with yourself the intent with which you do it. Intent is something different from conscious intention: intent is the purpose of following a greater design than we normally identify with individual will. It reflects one's spiritual destiny.

Other ways to find your own symbol(s) may come to mind and will certainly work for you. What our imagination suggests works because it is already part of reality.

Once you have found the symbol, you can begin to work with it, that is, to use it as a guide for reflection, meditation, and imagination.

I therefore recommend that you first start with the images in order to receive inspiration and their suggestions. Whether you choose the symbol in a divinatory way or based on aesthetic attraction or intuition, first look at the image and let it act (imagine, fantasize, think, reflect, meditate, visualize the symbol). Only after this would I recommend that you read the description of the symbol(s) and the phrases I received in meditation. They are just a blueprint—they may or may not correspond to you; what matters is that you then deepen them in your own way. These insights are personal and different for each of us. My directions on meditation should also be read after you take some time to sit with the symbols in this book, or you can ignore the descriptions and proceed in your own way.

However, as a guide, here is the outline I usually use to note my experiences with each symbol:

- This symbol tells me . . .

- This symbol takes me through . . .

- This symbol inspires me . . .

- I will color this symbol this way . . .

To work on the symbol, I suggest you allow yourself enough time to really let its meaning sink in and permeate your being, for at least an hour for each symbol. However, there are no limits: you can work on it for several months, years, lifetimes. You never stop discovering and learning.

I suggest you proceed as follows with each symbol you work with:

- Look at the symbol without focusing on the details and instead try to grasp the entire picture. You can use the original symbol that appears by each description, or you can go to Part 3 and view the full-size illustrations, where the symbol is embedded in imaginative content that has been inspired by my work with the symbols. These illustrations can suggest expansions of the essence of the symbol.

- Do not strive to immediately understand its meaning but simply look at it as an artistic piece, as you would look at a sunset or a flower, and let it suggest ideas, thoughts, emotions, and feelings.

- Then you can read my text or look elsewhere for traditional, religious, or esoteric meanings.

- Meditate on the symbol or allow yourself to be open to receiving its message.

- Reproduce it: draw it in whatever way you are inspired to.

- Use it as a guide: examine the reproduction you made and write a story or a poem or simple sentences about it.

- Color the symbol: This is a way to contribute to universal creativity and connect more with the symbols' deep meanings. Coloring the symbol is a beautiful sensory and imaginative exploration in which you immerse yourself in the symbol without thoughts, with an open heart, attentive only to your inner movements. You can photocopy the original illustrations in Part 3 and color them separately, or you can color directly in the book. You can hang up your colored drawing and look at it like a mandala, to relive within yourself the sensations that the symbol has given you, to discover new details and new images and find new explanations and suggestions, or for the simple pleasure of seeing it. Even colors have a symbolic value, which you can explore for yourself.

Visualization and Meditation on the Symbol

Symbolic images have a particular power to transport us immediately into the realm of sacred archetypes, connecting us with their energy field and infusing us with their qualities. Symbols are therefore a powerful tool for meditation—not a specific practice but the act of voluntarily emptying the mind of thoughts, emotions, and intellectual elaborations and leaving it free to access the subtle perceptions that reach beyond the limited sphere of our common sensory and intellectual experience.

Meditation is a state of openness in which we are receptive; that is, we are present but expanded and open. The prerequisite of meditation is physical and mental relaxation. Meditation is the opposite of the effort aimed at a specific goal: it means simply being present in the moment you are living. To get there, it is necessary to decondition oneself and at the same time tune in to higher and wider frequencies; it is an exercise in non-doing, the wu wei of Taoism, the creative mental void.

I stress again, it is important to empty your mind of thoughts and relax. It is good to be quiet and possibly alone in a peaceful place where you are comfortable. It is also helpful to enact a simple purification ritual, such as burning incense or wild sage (if that is within your tradition) or diffusing drops of water or a perfume, while you focus on your intent.

My advice is to start paying attention to your breathing, with your eyes closed, without forcing, without looking for a particular rhythm or type of inhalation or exhalation, simply letting the breath flow and observing it calmly. Find a comfortable position while sitting, with the back erect but not rigid, hands resting and relaxed in your lap, feet firmly placed on the floor. Next, open your eyes, without immediately focusing your gaze but letting it flow softly over the image. Then close your eyes again and visualize the symbol mentally, this time imagining it vividly in detail.

As it happens to me and as I have expressed in the drawings, other images often spring from the symbol and around it. It's like a dream, or rather, it's like when we spontaneously visualize the *persistent images*, which are those that appear when we close our eyes after staring very intensely at an object or the source of light itself. Persistent images are copies of the images we saw with our eyes open, especially the luminous ones. This occurs on a physical level, but on the subtle plane of inner perceptions, something similar often happens, namely the impression of what we have seen and experienced in the physical world is printed in our unconscious, and it remains there as an echo.

Once seen, the symbol remains in us: it is like the ripples that spread after a stone thrown into the water. Its presence modifies our inner space and transforms us, pushing us to a leap in consciousness.

It is a good idea to experiment with more than one symbol, if not all of those included in this book, to identify the one that best suits your current situation and the conditions in which you find yourself. The first symbol that arrives is the one that represents exactly what you must live and experience in the present moment, but exploring more than one will deepen the experience. In any case, after some time, different symbols may appear that correspond to the new situation we are experiencing and clarify it.

This form of practice with the sacred symbols does not imply betraying or abandoning one's faith or one's way of spiritual search. The symbol itself is only a means to enter the sacred, which is a dimension beyond any belief. Many different paths can be followed to reach the summit.

Reproducing the Symbols

Drawing the symbols is a way to absorb and project their power. You can draw the symbols either in the spur of the moment or in a more meditative way—using pencil or in color—and on paper or even digitally on a tablet or computer.

The symbols can be drawn or reproduced on a vase, container, plate, glass, bottle, piece of furniture, cell phone case, pretty much anywhere—the qualities of the symbols thus enter our daily lives, pouring their power into the food we eat, the actions we perform, the relationships we have with others, and every moment of our lives. I highly suggest reproducing the symbols on the objects and tools found and used in the kitchen, so the food that enters you is charged with the virtues and energetic vibrations of the symbols.

Another way is to *create an object that depicts a symbol*. You can use modeling clay or air-dry clay (found online and in art supply stores), or you can use natural elements or those found in everyday life such as wood, stones, pens, shells, ropes, paper, pasta, seeds and grains, or anything that your imagination suggests. Embrace your inner-child artist! Creating something with found items is what we all used to do as children: it's an act of becoming young again in order to move forward and evolve. Those who are more skilled with their hands or who have craft skills can reproduce the symbols by creating a pendant or an artistic object, such as with wood.

Drawing the symbols on mirrors in your home with dry erase markers or even lipstick is another way to let their power penetrate you as you look at your reflection.

Other ways to bring the symbols to life is on your own body through *body painting* or *tattooing*. Body painting is obviously less permanent than a tattoo; if you don't like the idea of having an indelible marking on your body, you can still make a temporary tattoo with erasable materials.

Another way to reproduce a symbol is through a *gesture*. When you trace it in the air, the symbol gains more strength in your subconscious.

An even more effective way to become attuned to a symbol is to reproduce it physically with your body in its entirety: it is a spiritual manifestation and mimicry that transfers the quality of the symbol into the person experiencing it. Many Eastern energy disciplines, from yoga to Chinese qigong, use the body as a vehicle for this symbolic work by reproducing natural elements, animals, plants, and movements of energy. The dances and traditional ceremonies of Indigenous peoples have the same value. In working with the sacred symbols found in this book, if say the Cross appears or resonates with you, you could reproduce the shape with your arms raised. If the Ensō appears, you can invite a person

to embrace and breathe with you, alternating exhalation and inhalation (while one inhales the other exhales). If the Udjat, the Eye of Horus, appears, you might try looking away into the far-off distance, immobilizing yourself and focusing your sight on a very distant point, mimicking a hawk in the hunt that has spotted prey. If the Dot and Circle appears, you can make a circle with your arms or bend your body into a semicircle position. If the Labyrinth appears, you could move around the room as if you were inside a labyrinth. If the Goddess appears, with your hand you can trace a spiral that starts from your navel and expands outward and beyond the boundaries of your body, and so on. In short, it is a matter of physically reproducing the symbol in some way, of letting it come to life in you and listening to the modifications and indications that you receive from your intuition. The sensations you feel and the perceptions you get can be very strong and immediate and have clarity and evidence, but they can also be indefinite, almost ineffable or unclear, like oracular verdicts which we must then investigate (for the most important ones, sometimes it can take years).

In any case I suggest you write down (or draw) all these suggestions, intuitions, and sensations immediately after the experience. Even if they are immediately clear, their meaning must be explored further to refine and distill an even deeper and more subtle meaning. I recommend keeping a notebook dedicated exclusively to this work, in which to collect your experiences, but there is also a space next to each full-size illustration in Part 3 for writing down your observations.

Recording Messages, Evoking, and Representing the Symbol

The *visualization* of the symbol and the *meditation* inspired by it are experiences that bring a great harvest of imaginative, psychic, and spiritual contents. My advice is to immediately write (or draw or verbally record) what you receive, just as you would do with dreams or ideas that come suddenly, to help yourself remember them and thus be able to evoke and use them for inner guidance. You can transcribe the messages you receive from your intuition in the form of simple notes or you can express them in artistic form—reflections inspired by the symbol. For example, you could write short poems in the style of a Japanese haiku, a short and essential composition of two or three sentences. Or in the future, when visualizing or meditating on a symbol for a second time, you can examine what messages or input you receive in light of the subsequent events and/or developments since the last time you worked with the symbol, and make comparisons between the current and past revelations received.

The symbol can also *inspire a story or allegory*, as I have expressed graphically in the full-size illustrations in Part 3. To those who are artists, it can suggest a song, a flower arrangement, a sculpture, a dance step or an entire choreography, a dialogue or theater piece, or even an architectural design.

To those who work in education, training, or assistance to people, those who are therapists, counselors, or coaches, the symbol may suggest action strategies and solutions for the cases they are working on.

It is also very effective to share one's experiences with friends, acquaintances, confidants, and collaborators: talking with others—comparing and exchanging impressions and stories—is a way to reinforce and consolidate one's insights, to reinforce and circulate the energy that has been set in motion, and to learn and grow together with others. By working with one another on the symbols in some way, you can combine the exploration of the symbol with divination.

Having attuned with a certain symbol and having begun to work on it, you will inevitably and increasingly notice it in your daily life, recognizing it even where you do not expect to. Maybe you've passed by it many times without noticing, distracted by the mental chatter or daily gossip, and losing sight of the essential. At this point you can contemplate the symbol with a more conscious consideration and perhaps even photograph it on your phone so that you may always be able to reflect on the presence of these important signs whenever and wherever, in every aspect of your life. A cross symbol drawn on a wall, a four-leaf clover in your yard, a cloud floating above, a stone with a particular shape, a tree outside your office, a pattern in a woman's dress, an animal that runs across your path—everything becomes a symbol of the living soul, every sign gives you a precise message, appropriate to the moment you are living and precious for your evolution.

The ideal conclusion of this path is to find and draw your own personal symbol that expresses your deepest self and personality. You can also create a *collective symbol*—a symbol that represents your family, your community, the whole of humanity, or even planet Earth. The point of this exercise is to have fun but to also share this new image with others and communicate what your vision is for your personal symbol. Just as graphic designers attempt to do today with logo designs, what is the story and message you are trying to convey with your collective symbol? Be creative and fearless. Even if something already exists that is similar to what you created, every symbol that is born is like a new flower: unique, indispensable, current, useful, fertile, and wonderful.

Part 2

Sacred Symbols

The symbols mentioned in this book belong to different cultural areas and different spiritual or esoteric strands. Some go beyond categories (geographical, cultural, religious, and spiritual) and are universal: the Dot and Circle, the Spiral, the Labyrinth, the Mask, the Cross, the Sword, the Goddess. In some cases, such as the Cross, particular religions or spiritual paths have made symbols their own.

Some symbols come from specific geographical and cultural areas; others have been adopted by communities as distinctive elements. From pre-Columbian and Indigenous America come the Kapemni of the Lakota, the Totem Pole of the coastal tribes of the Pacific Northwest, the glyphs of the Maya calendar systems, and the Incan Chakana; from Oceania come the Mata Komoe of the Marquesas Islands and the Tjurunga of the First Peoples of Australia; from Japan, the Zen circle Ensō and the Torii; from China, the Bagua (with a taijitu); from Tibet, the Dorje; from India and Tibet, the Kolovrat; from Buddhism, the Dharmachakra, the wheel of the law; from India, the Om and the Lingam-Yoni; from ancient Persia, the Faravahar; from West Africa, the Nyame Ye Ohene; from ancient Egypt, the Ankh (the crux ansata), and the Udjat, the Eye of Horus.

To the Islamic area belong the Crescent Moon as well as the Khamsa, or the hand of Fatima; to the primitive Christianity, Ichthýs, the fish of Christ; to Judaism, the Māgēn Dāwīd, the Seal of Solomon; to the area of the ancient Minoan and Greek civilizations belong the Labrys (the bipennis axe) and the Caduceus; to the prehistoric Italic populations and their rock engravings belong the Camunian Rose and the divinatory Etruscan Liver and Mirror; to the Italian Renaissance, the Vitruvian Man; to the peoples of Northern and Eastern Europe, the Valknut and the Runes of the Norse, the Vegvísir of the Vikings, the Celtic Triskele, the Beaivi of the Sámi, and the Kolovrat of the Slavs.

To the hermetic and alchemical tradition can be traced the Ouroboros, the Alchemical Pot, and the Etz Hayim, or the kabbalistic tree of life.

Infinity is a symbol of another kind, not properly sacred but referring to the mathematical sciences. However, even this symbol represents the point where our rational and analytical minds confront the mystery that mathematics can only illustrate with an image that is not calculable and measurable, it being beyond our human understanding.

1

KAPEMNI

The Mirror of the Universe on Earth

Celebrate with a ceremony to remember your place in the world.

KEYWORD: CONNECTION

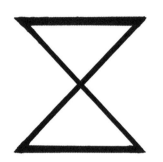

The sky is our home as much as the earth, which is also part of the sky and follows its motions. According to the Lakota people, also known as the Teton Sioux, who are just one of the many Indigenous tribes of America, we come from the stars, and we live on this earth reproducing the stars' motions. The two cones depicted in the Kapemni are tipis, represented schematically to express the meeting between the celestial sphere and the terrestrial sphere. Our tipi is both on earth and in heaven; there is a continuous exchange of energies between the high (the divine) and the low (the human world). Where they meet flows the woniya, the breath of Wakan Tanka, the Great Mystery. The Lakota followed it on earth and celebrated it in sacred ceremonies and in the yearly pilgrimages they undertook on the prairies where they hunted bison and established their camps.

You are an embodied spirit, and here on earth you continue a boundless journey that began long ago and far away and will go on beyond any apparent end. Mitákuye Oyás'iŋ, which is a Lakota prayer that means "We are all related."

2
TOTEM POLE
The Great Living Family

Honor all life and stand firm.

KEYWORD: BELONGING

We are part of the great family that includes the entire cosmos and all living things. Life is bigger than our individual existence and contains us. Plants, animals, natural elements are perpetuated within us: we carry and transport their memory into the present and the future. We are brothers and sisters, sons and daughters, fathers and mothers, grandfathers and grandmothers, ancestors and descendants, heirs and guardians of all living forms. Totem Poles are made from tree trunks and represent family trees, depicting family lineages and clans, family crests in the form of animals, and ancestors, and they tell ancestral stories. They were and are created by the coastal Indigenous cultures of the Pacific Northwest in North America.

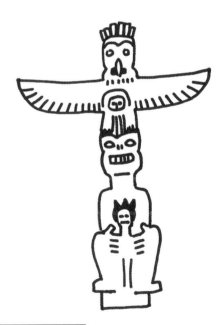

Thank your ancestors and those who have gone before you and pray for your descendants and those yet to be born, for all the creatures who accompany you, who care for you, and who need you.

3

TZOLK'IN AND HAAB
The Maya Calendar

Make time your ally.

KEYWORD: DURATION

We study, measure, and represent time to become attuned to cosmic rhythms and to master our earthly existence. We celebrate it with ceremonies to bring the sacred quality of harmony into daily life.

For the Maya of ancient pre-Columbian Central America, there were three cycles of time, intertwined with each other and dominated by the divine powers: a ritual and sacred calendar (Tzolk'in) of 260 days; the solar calendar of 365 days (Haab, with the last five days being unlucky and for rest); and a Long Count calendar that measured the great eras, or approximately 5,125 years. The three cycles—the sacred one, the solar one, and the great one—fit together like the cogwheels of an immense cosmic mechanism, making time and lives flow.

When you're struggling with inner transformations that require patience and foresight, wait. When it's time to face the new reality, act.

4
CHAKANA
The Andean Cross

Explore all your realities and possibilities.

KEYWORD: INTERDEPENDENCE

The three steps of each corner of the Chakana represent heaven, earth, and underworld, the three levels of the cosmos for the ancient Incas. The guardians of the three worlds are the condor, the puma, and the snake, respectively. Representing the universe at the center of the cross is the circle, or cusco (meaning "navel," as the capital city of Cusco was the heart of the world for the Andean people). The arms of the cross represent the cardinal points, the twelve corners the months of the year, and the whole symbol recalls the sacred Southern Cross constellation as the four stars indicate the cardinal point in that hemisphere. The Chakana (meaning "to bridge" and "to cross over") connects the universe with all the life within it.

In all your decisions and actions, keep in mind all the planes of existence: the heavenly, the earthly, and the hidden underworld. You belong to all three worlds—together they form the reality of life.

5
MATA KOMOE*
The Sign of Value

Show your value.

KEYWORD: COURAGE

The body is the first expression of art and spirit. In the islands of the Pacific, the body was used for artistic decorations and to express spiritual beliefs, social rank, and lineage. Through the evidence of body carving, one's value was demonstrated, and beauty, physical attractiveness, and charm were exalted. Mata Komoe, or "death's head," in the tattoos of the people of the Marquesas Islands, the home of this art, marked the bodies of victorious warriors to honor their virtues of strength and courage.

Assert your personality. Express yourself and all your strength without restraint or hesitation to overcome the arduous trials we all undergo.

---

* Georg Heinrich von Langsdorff, Bemerkungen auf einer Reise um die Welt in den Jahren 1803 bis 1807 (Frankfurt, Germany: Friedrich Wilmans, 1812–1814), https://natlib.govt.nz/records/22805879.

6
TJURUNGA
The Dreamtime Map

Draw on the most ancient knowledge and stories.

KEYWORD: PATH

Australian Aboriginal groups had sacred familial totem objects called the Tjurungas, also known as Churingas, that were secretly guarded and used as spiritual navigators. Engraved on the stone or wood were sacred designs that represented the journey and the encounters made by the ancestors in the alcheringa, the Dreamtime, the mythical era in which the ancestral spirits shaped the world by singing. A Tjurunga symbolizes the map of the soul so one may find and follow the songlines, the spiritual routes along which the Aboriginal Peoples walk, pray, and sing the ancient sacred songs in rituals that keep the world alive by renewing creation.

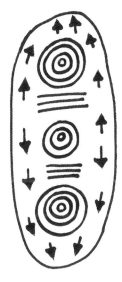

Bring to light what you have kept hidden. Evaluate the origins and implications of your past choices and actions. In light of this reflection, determine your current position and bring your creative contribution to life.

7

ENSŌ
The Zen Circle

Prepare and meditate to give
yourself over to life.

KEYWORD: PERFECTION

A moment is as perfect as the circle—it contains all worlds. Drawn on rice paper or silk with a single gesture without premeditation or second thoughts, Ensō (円相 in kanji ideograms) is the circle that also serves as the signature of the works of Japanese Zen masters. Open or closed, compact or fragmentary, dense or tenuous, it represents the absolute and strength—the signature of the Spirit through the human hand. It expresses the balance between spontaneity and intellect achieved through preparation and meditation. It designates the goal of the spiritual seeker: the lasting state of enlightenment called satori in which one is at one with natural forces. In nature, it is bamboo that meets these requirements: circular and hollow as well as solid and strong, elegant and simple, capable of bending as well as acting as a building material.

Without forcing it, abandon your expectations and remove the superfluous. Wait and be humble and honest with yourself, but when you have to act, be free and immediate, fluid and unpredictable, decisive and timely.

8
TORII
The Sacred Portal

Step out of your daily routine
to find yourself.

KEYWORD: CONTEMPLATION

There is a threshold beyond which we are in the divine, where what is matter becomes spirit and vice versa. A Torii is a gateway or portal in front of shrines or places where there are kami, the spirits of nature of the traditional Japanese Shinto religion. It represents, with its two vertical pillars capped by horizontal beams, the gateway through which one passes, purifying oneself, from the profane to a sacred space. It is at the same time a representation of the legend of the Goddess of the Sun, Amaterasu: after she hid in a cave on Mount Fuji, causing an eclipse, men placed a large perch before the cave's entrance to gather the birds, which intrigued her, and their singing called her out of the cave, bringing back the sun. This is reflected in the kanji of the word *Torii* in Japanese (鳥居), which mean "bird" and "existence."

As soon as you can, leave the frenzy of tasks in which you hide and lose yourself, so you may purify and restore yourself. Simply walk free in the light of the sun to better live your commitments in harmony with others.

9

BAGUA

The Flow of Energies

Find harmony beyond
the apparent opposition.

KEYWORD: BALANCE

Balance comes from the alternation and relationship between two complementary poles. In everything there is an opposite: in the dark night, the light moon; in the bright day, the shadow; in life, death; and vice versa, as in the disease, the healing; in health, the disease. Each of the two polarities carries within itself the essence of the other: this is the reality of energy and physical life.

In Chinese, *Bagua* (八卦) means "eight symbols." It is the map of cosmic and natural energies. In the center there is the taijitu of Taoist spirituality, which is the graphic expression of the union of complementary opposites (yin feminine energy, night, shadow, passivity, negativity; yang masculine energy, daytime, light, activity, positivity). The same complementary opposition of empty-full is in the trigrams of whole or broken lines surrounding the yin-yang symbol, which are tools of divination in the oracular *I Ching* book. The Bagua is also a symbol of feng shui, the art of harmonizing the energies of the home and the environment.

Don't judge things by their initial appearance—nothing is static, everything is constantly moving and changing. Pay attention to the shadows as well as the light, the problems as well as the opportunities. In every situation, there is a possible alternative.

10

DORJE

The Purity of Mind

Be devoted and happy, don't get attached to anything: life is a moment.

KEYWORD: MEDITATION

Enlightenment and spiritual strength, the purest teachings of the Buddha who eradicates ignorance, are the male side of the spiritual quest represented in the Dorje (or *vajra* in Sanskrit, which is related to the words for *diamond* and *thunderbolt*). In sacred images, the Buddha holds the Dorje in his right hand while the bell—*ghanta* in Sanskrit—is held in the left and represents the feminine, the body. The double structure of the Dorje also alludes to the union of spiritual truth (Nirvana) with the painful repeating cycle of life and death (samsara). Often two crossed Dorje are represented, one open and the other one closed (alluding to the peaceful and angry states of the divinity), at the center of mandalas, which are the cosmic representations used as a support for meditation.

The mantra represented in Tibetan letters on the illustration is Om mani padme hum ("O jewel on the lotus flower, grant me all realizations"), a mantra of the bodhisattva of compassion to ask for the purification of body, speech, and mind.

Combine kindness with strength to achieve serenity by which you can see clearly what your true goals are. Rid yourself of indecision and find the essence of things.

11

DHARMACHAKRA

The Wheel of the Law

Take responsibility to interrupt
the endless cycle of mistakes.

KEYWORD: EQUANIMITY

This material world is driven by desire and hatred. The law of cause and effect, karma, makes our existence turn like a wheel. After detaching from desires and self-serving habits, the enlightened person comes out of this vortex of illusions, no longer being endlessly reincarnated, and accesses Nirvana, the pure consciousness beyond time and space at the

center of the wheel, disciplined and motionless. The Wheel of Eight Spokes is the new law established by the Buddha (Dharma) to establish a new era in human life where compassion takes the place of the passions. The eight spokes represent his message, contained in the Noble Eightfold Path (right view, right intention, right speech, right action, right livelihood, right effort, right mindfulness, right concentration), which leads from suffering to salvation.

Think: "What am I living, what am I doing, where are my actions taking me?" Take charge of your life and abandon the deceptions of the mind and senses to adhere to your deepest truth.

12
OM
The Creative Vibration

Rediscover your core self.

KEYWORD: UNITY

Everybody, everything that exists, emerges from the divine vibration. In the Indian tradition, Om is the primordial sound (Pranava mantra) that pervades the entire universe, manifesting the divine. It is also called a bīja mantra, or the "seed-sound" that originates everything. Om means (among other things) the union of the three aspects of divinity (creation, preservation, and destruction-renewal) expressed by the letters *A* and *U* (which together become *O*) and *M*. The graphic symbol for Om also represents the primary states of consciousness (waking, dream, and deep sleep) and the planes of existence (physical, mental, and spiritual). The chanting of Om harmonizes them, renews the connection with the infinite original source, and thus removes obstacles to the realization of the individual self.

Stop, close your eyes, breathe, and listen to the sound of your body, express it. It is your inner voice from which flow all the possibilities for a life full of satisfaction.

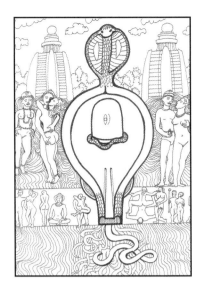

13

LINGAM-YONI
The Cosmic Union

Enjoy every aspect of life with
confidence and devotion.

KEYWORD: JOY

Male and female are the two aspects of the divine that unite in a sacred embrace in which the universe is generated. Sexual union is one of its earthly manifestations. Pleasure, love, and attraction are part of the cosmic game of the gods, lila, and the creative illusion, maya, with which we experience separation and reunification. In the sacred union of maithuna, the sexual coupling is seen as a dance that leads souls into life and thus manifests the divine. The senses and every single element, every act of life, are steps on the ladder that leads back to the undifferentiated infinite. Tantra, the esoteric strand of yoga, celebrates all of existence as a sacrament. The symbol represents the male energy (the god Shiva, Lingam) in union with the female energy (the goddess Shakti, Yoni). The serpent is the universal energy condensed and made body, blood, and drive.

Recognize the importance of every moment and everything you do. Everything is sacred. Bliss permeates your entire existence.

14

FARAVAHAR

The Pact with Goodwill

Let the greater good guide you.

KEYWORD: DISCERNMENT

Humans are free to let Sepanta Minu (positive force) prevail over their Ankareh Minu (negative force) through "Good thoughts, good words, and good deeds." These pillars allow one to rise, to choose the good and set aside the evil. They are the practical principles of the religion founded by the Persian prophet Zarathustra (or Zoroaster), still alive in the Parsi community, which sees the world divided between good (God, Ahura Mazdā) and evil (Angra Mainyu). The winged being who guides us rises above malevolence and makes a pact (symbolized by the ring) with the spirit (the circle). In this covenant resides peace, goodness, and eternal life. It was the emblem of the ancient Persian empire.

Trust in the highest principles. When in doubt, ask yourself, "Is what I'm sensing good for me and for others?" Put your faith in your inner truth.

15

MĀGĒN DĀWĪD

The Seal of Solomon

Adjust your every thought and action
by placing them in a divine space.

KEYWORD: ORDER

Spirit and matter are united, intertwined, and allied. The two opposing equilateral triangles with the points facing upward and downward represent the high, spiritual elements (air and fire) and the material ones (earth and water), respectively, of which the heart is born in the center. Defined in esotericism as the Seal of Solomon, the six-pointed star, or hexagram, is also known as Star or Shield of David. In Hebrew it is named מגן דוד (Māgēn Dāwīd), but it is also present in other traditions. In the center is reproduced the name of God in Hebrew characters: the tetragrammaton (a Greek word that means "four letters"), יהוה (JHVH, or Yahweh). The letters of the Hebrew alphabet are direct emanations of the divinity, but words are a trace of the spirit, they cannot define it.

Keep faith and confidence even when every circumstance seems adverse and confusing. Even if you cannot know and understand everything, persevere and you will be complete.

16

ETZ HAYIM
The Tree of Life

Follow your inner light.

KEYWORD: STUDY

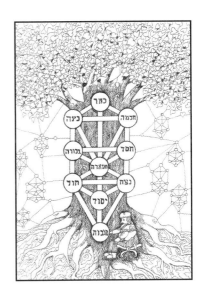

Infinite God, the unlimited unknowable light (*Ohr Ein Sof* in Kabbalah), beyond space and time and all possible human knowledge, manifests itself in our world through the ten emanations (Sephirot). Its essential qualities are the original instructions that govern our existence. It is a mystical tree that has roots in heaven and grows on earth, transferring in creation—like sap in the tree—the divine powers. Its structure is solid and splendid and bears as fruits the sacred letters of the alphabet, the keys to knowledge. The initiate to the esoteric tradition of Jewish Kabbalah studies the Tree of Life, Etz Hayim (עץ חיים in Hebrew), to understand and translate the language of God and apply its teachings.

Investigate nature, physical reality, and inner reality to understand the Spirit and to read and interpret the arcane language in which the divine expresses itself.

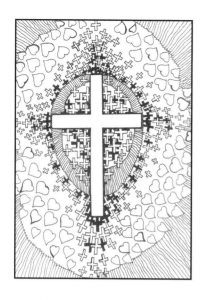

17

CROSS

The Meeting in the Heart

Rebirth: give up your fears
and start over.

KEYWORD: SACRIFICE

The heart is the center from which universal and unconditional love flows and radiates. The Cross is divine love on earth, the ascent beyond the suffering of living. In every part of the world, the cross represents the meeting and the union of heaven and earth, of divine and human, of spirit and matter, which meet in the heart. Here, the human being, the Son, in Christianity, is born. In Christianity it is the sign that symbolizes the death and resurrection of Christ, the sacrifice in which the pain of the separation from the Father is transformed into a symbol of joy, fulfillment, fullness. *Sacrifice* means "to make sacred"; it does not mean only pain but change and renewal.

Sacrifice illusions but keep hope in life. Stand in truth and trust in love: you are not separate from others; you are one with the universe.

18

ICHTHÝS

The Fish of Christ

Keep quiet about your innermost faith.

KEYWORD: CAUTION

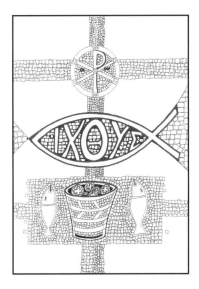

At times hidden and secret, as if underwater, mute but darting like a fish, faith in the living God saves and works miracles. The fish (ἰχθύς, *ikhthŭs* in ancient Greek) is a Christogram, one of the symbols created by the early Christians in a time of persecution. It's an acronym that, in Greek, stands for Ἰησοῦς Χριστός Θεοῦ Υἱός Σωτήρ (Iesùs CHristòs THeù HYiòs Sotèr; or Jesus Christ, Son of God, Savior). By drawing one half of it, the faithful could recognize the coreligionists who knew how

to complete it: it is a symbol in the literal sense of the term as it unites two halves. Perhaps it alludes to the apostles who were fishermen (Peter and Andrew, the fishers of men), to the miracle of the multiplication of the loaves and fishes, and thus to the increase of the faithful through preaching.

Even in the riskiest circumstances, what you believe in will come to pass. You will have your prize and be saved along with others if you share your secret with those who can recognize it.

19
CRESCENT MOON
The Light of the Soul

It's dawn—contemplate the beauty
of the sky and its revelations.

KEYWORD: FAITH

In the darkness of the soul shines the divine light, which illuminates and defeats the darkness of ignorance and disbelief. The crescent moon with the five-pointed star (هلال, *Hilāl* in Arabic) was a pre-Islamic symbol of the Byzantine Empire (the crescent moon was a symbol of the goddess Artemis, protector of the ancient Greek Byzantium). Adopted by the Ottomans at the conquest of Constantinople, it later became the sign of the power and victory of Islam and appears on many flags of Muslim states. The five-pointed star represents the Prophet Muhammad, whose name written in Arabic appears as a five-pointed star.

In heaven, your path and destiny are clearly marked out, and you can choose to conform by submitting to divinity. It is a new beginning; begin now to accomplish your work with confidence.

20

KHAMSA

The Hand of Fatima

Safeguard your inner calm, your intimacy, and your affections.

KEYWORD: PROTECTION

Faith gives comfort and good fortune. It shows the true love of God. It protects against bad luck, jealousy, and agitation. Strength and self-discipline allow one to master passions and attachments and give prosperity and peace. Called the Hand of Fatima, Hamsa (or Khamsa), (خَمْسَة, in Arabic) means "five" as in the fingers of the hand, the five pillars of Islam, and the five senses through which human beings relate to the world. It represents the hand of a woman, Fatima, the daughter of the Prophet, who was cooking when her husband and his new wife appeared. So affected by this surprise, Fatima dropped the ladle but continued stirring with her hand, not noticing it was burning. When she pulled it out of the pot, she saw her hand had two thumbs, a miracle. Seeing this, it is said that her husband put aside his new wife and devoted himself to Fatima. The eye signifies faith and knowledge of God. It is also a Jewish symbol (the Hand of Miriam, sister of Moses and Aaron, and a symbol of the five books of the Torah) and of other cultures.

Control your impulses to defend what is most dear to you. Trust in the assistance of spiritual forces, which know how to help you and work to protect what is right and pure.

21
ANKH
The Key to Eternal Life

Take charge of your destiny.

KEYWORD: CONTINUITY

The Ankh (the *crux ansata* in Latin) was known as the key of life in ancient Egypt and was often depicted in art within the hands of the gods who govern human affairs, symbolizing the key that opens the doors of immortality. The Egyptian pharaohs intended to live beyond physical death through a rebirth, an ancestral aspiration of many cultures. The Ankh represents the union between the human and divine world, between male and female, between heaven and earth. It is the ancestor of the symbol of the Cross. To some, it represents the rising sun, to others the Nile that gives life on earth. The union of sun and air, earth and water, the elements that all living things need.

Fear nothing. You are never alone, and you will not disappear even with death, because you are living light; you will always be part of the universe. You will continue to exist. Death and adversity in life can do nothing against your existence.

22

UDJAT
The Eye of Horus

Stay open to new points of view without preconceived notions.

KEYWORD: VISION

We are light incarnate and will continue to be so even after physical death. Over our earthly path watches the god Horus, the falcon-headed sky deity of proverbial sight. Seeing the light outside of ourselves allows us to recognize it, in a mirror, within us. This makes us humans a conscious part of nature, sharing some divine attributes. Light is also immortality: the source of life, God, or whichever being shows up in your faith, is not subject to disappearance as it is eternal and ageless, unlike the shadows it casts in the world. The all-seeing eye is often associated with the ancient Egyptian Udjat but is present in many cultures. The Udjat symbol represents the eye of Horus and the moon but is also sometimes known as the eye of Ra, the sun god. It is a sign of royalty, prosperity, and health.

Look at things from above as if for the first time. Like a bird in flight, detach yourself from earthly limitations. You will see clearly, as if by magic, the solution to your problems and obtain peace and harmony.

23

MASK
The True Face

There's no need to identify
with what you currently think and
are—you are so much more.

KEYWORD: REVELATION

The mask is our true face: whoever wears it embodies beings present not in physical form but spirits on the incorporeal plane. It shows in visible, symbolic form our belonging to the divine world. It hides the personal identity of the wearer while manifesting the spiritual essence. We are not people who possess souls; we are souls who travel in material forms in the physical world wearing temporary "masks" made of individual personalities, bodies, family histories. Our true nature reveals itself when we undress from the ego and feel part of the whole existence.

The symbol of the mask is still present and significant in Africa and other non-Western cultures, but it can be found throughout the world and in all times (from ancient Greek theater to carnival and ritual performances). It symbolizes going beyond known individuality to reveal the unknown.

Put yourself at the service of an ancient power, greater than you can imagine. All of existence, the legacy of your ancestors, the incorporeal spirits, and the evolution of the whole world are manifested through you.

24

NYAME YE OHENE
Divine Sovereignty

Honor the divine power and royal strength that pervades every living thing.

KEYWORD: AUTHORITY

One of the most important symbols of the Asante people of Ghana, West Africa, represents the majesty of God. *Nyame Ye Ohene* translates to "God is King." Omnipresent, omniscient, the divine dominates all creation and is manifested in all things. The sign manifests our presence in life and reminds us that we are immersed in the divine. The shapes in the center are the stylization of the knuckles of a fist, a gesture that signifies keeping life under control and in one's power.

It is one of the Adinkra, a complex figurative language of symbols from Ghana with which stories, concepts, and proverbs are communicated in a visual form to send greetings and salutations and share ideas and feelings. In West Africa, they are found everywhere: on clothes, on walls, and in homes.

To be like royalty, recognize the best qualities in each person, and reward and encourage them to embrace their regal lineage as well.

25

LABYRINTH

The Inner Journey

Tackle even the most complex and intricate situations with decision and courage.

KEYWORD: INITIATION

In order to know ourselves, we must lose and find ourselves again. Once arriving at the center of our Labyrinth, we can return to the world. The Labyrinth can represent bewilderment and confusion; not knowing where you are going makes you fall into fear. But entering the Labyrinth also means strength (the hero who penetrates it), faith (the pilgrim who enters it to meditate), hope (the Greek's Ariadne, whose thread helps us get out), victory (over the evil that lurks in the background), orientation, and decision.

The Labyrinth is of two types: the maze, with dead-end paths and deception, and the circular labyrinth, like that of Chartres Cathedral in France in which you cannot get lost or be deceived if you rely on God—here there are no detours or possible illusions.

You will know who you are by the choices you make. Your intelligence and your thoughts, your emotions and your feelings, as well as your sensitivity will guide you with the prodigious help of the spirit.

26

LABRYS

The Bipennis Axe

Take charge of your power
without fear or arrogance.

KEYWORD: POWER

The creative power of the mother goddess is two sided, like the double-bitted axe: she gives both life and death; she cuts down vegetation and sacrifices bulls to nourish and protect her people. The deity holds in her hands the opposing forces of creation and destruction as a sign of her power. In the ancient Minoan civilization of Crete, the goddess held snakes, which also represent death and rebirth. The two-headed axe entered Greek and Roman cultures as a male symbol: the primitive gylany, the culture in which the two sexes were in balance, was replaced by the patriarchal kingdom in which strength became oppression. Today we are once again beginning to recognize and honor nonviolence, acceptance, and understanding: the life-giving, matriarchal aspects of power.

Fairness and detachment will help you receive what you believe is right for you. Control and decision are one with tranquility and kindness.

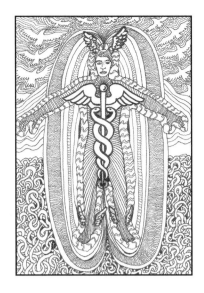

27

CADUCEUS
The Divine Messenger

Turn snake venom into medicine.

KEYWORD: TRANSFORMATION

The winged divine intelligence holds together and harmonizes opposites, giving well-being and health. From the Greek word *karykeion*, Caduceus means "divine messenger." It was a symbol of the god Hermes (known as Mercury to the Romans), herald of the gods, who interrupted a fight between two snakes by throwing between them a golden staff given to him by Apollo, god of reason and light that illuminates the intellect. A symbol of prosperity and peace in antiquity, it is now the symbol of medicine that cures the human being by mastering changes and restoring balance thanks to the knowledge of natural laws. It also resembles the double helix of DNA: the source of life and its continuity.

Process your negativity and turn obstacles, conflicts, and problems into healing energy. What seems to hurt you can be a healthy resource; your flaws can be your strength.

28
THE GODDESS
The Divine Feminine

Respect and follow the cycles of life.

KEYWORD: FERTILITY

Next to the male divinity there is the Goddess, the feminine aspect of the sacred natural. She follows the lunar laws of change, of the phases of growth and decrease. She is the source of all living things, which all return to her eventually. Her beauty is creativity and fullness. Her body is the earthly manifestation of heaven, of which she is mother, daughter, companion, wife, lover. Her exuberance, elegance and harmony, and natural beauty are particularly connected to water and vegetation. In the present era, this symbol expresses the rebirth of the strength and sacred magic of the feminine.

Listen to the subtle and delicate moods and messages of nature. Be welcoming, tender, and creative as a woman who gives life and cherishes the gift of creation.

29

CAMUNIAN ROSE

The Memory of the World

Draw on the original instructions for living in harmony with others.

KEYWORD: COMMUNITY

The sun gives life to humanity and unites cultures. The essential events of life are inscribed forever on the stones in ancient engravings. Illuminated by the sun, the cliffs preserve and tell ancestral memories. The stones are the bones of the earth, on which human beings build their existence and their history. The Camunian Rose, thought to be a solar symbol to the ancient Camuni people, is one of the most famous prehistoric rock engraving designs of Val Camonica in Lombardy, Italy, appearing ninety-two times among the more than three hundred thousand rock carvings found there and dating back to the Iron Age. It is also present in many other sites, engravings, and ancient cultures all over the world.

The fundamental teachings were given to us long ago and are engraved forever in the substance of our lives. Respect simplicity even if it appears harsh and bare to you, for on the contrary, it is the ultimate refinement, an eternal guarantee of health and respect for others.

30

ETRUSCAN LIVER AND MIRROR
The Oracular Signs

Learn to decipher the signals
the universe sends you.

KEYWORD: CONSCIOUSNESS

We can see on earth what is in heaven, and in heaven what is on earth. The map of the cosmos is reproduced and reflected in the Etruscan Liver, an artifact found near Piacenza, Italy. It is the divinatory instrument on which the sacred areas of the universe are traced. There, the names of the divinities and of the corresponding spiritual forces are inscribed. The haruspices, those oracles of old, read signs and omens in animal entrails, using this representation as a guide.

The Etruscan bronze mirrors, inscribed on the back with sacred images and characters, were also a means to reveal the magic of the world, which is an inverted image—true and false at the same time—of ourselves.

The world is your mirror, and you are the world's mirror. When you open yourself up to the world, it clearly tells you who you are, where you are, and what you can and should do.

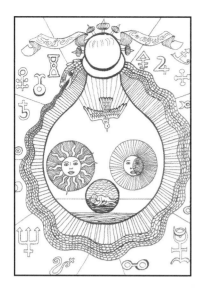

31

OUROBOROS AND THE ALCHEMICAL POT

Transmutation through Time and Space

Gather deep within the earth to expand.

KEYWORD: COMPLETION

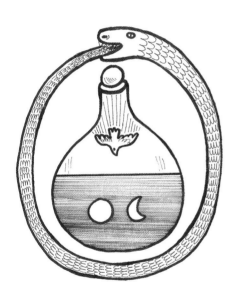

In the alchemical work, opposites come together. The Ouroboros serpent wraps around everything that exists and eats itself tail first, symbolizing how life and nature are perpetually in metamorphosis. In the Alchemical Pot (*vas hermetis* in Latin), matter is spiritualized, and the spirit is incarnated. It is an uninterrupted and admirable cycle. Alchemy is the work of transmutation that takes place simultaneously on the physical and spiritual plane and which is often aimed at the creation of an elixir of immortality. Its symbols express the phases and passages of the inner transformations: the Alchemical Pot is the cosmic womb, the serpent is time, the Athanor—the crucible—is the place of transformation.

Embrace heavenly inspiration like a seed. Let it sprout by trusting in time. You will be transformed, becoming all that you can be and doing all that you can do.

32

VITRUVIAN MAN
At the Center of the World

*Stand up for yourself;
show what you are and know.*

KEYWORD: DIGNITY

Man is the measure of all things. He emerges from nature as order from chaos. In him, earth and heaven, high and low, cosmos and microcosm, movement and stability, and unconscious and consciousness harmoniously meet. The circle and the square represent heaven and earth, infinite and finite, soul and body, respectively.

Leonardo da Vinci expressed the strength and confidence of Renaissance humanity through his drawing, in which faith, art, and science were united in a new synthesis. Man returned to the center of the world created by God, as his manifestation and as an instrument to realize his projects.

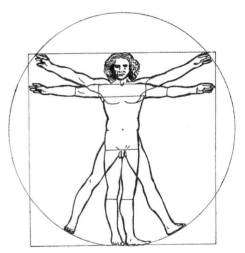

Recognize and embody your own qualities and recognize and respect them in others. Act with mastery, confidence, and self-esteem. Honor and celebrate human nature, which is complete in itself.

33

TRISKELE
The Triple Spiral

Seize the union between all aspects of life, even the "negative" ones.

KEYWORD: FLOW

Life expresses and evolves, moving from a center and returning to it according to a regular rhythm and in intertwined and interconnected circles. Body, mind, and spirit circulate in a single flow, creating fields of form that generate and shape existence. Triskele (from the Greek word *triskelés* for "three-legged"), the triple spiral, represents the expansion and manifestation of life in aspects of three: the three ages; the phases of the day and the moon; the components of the human being (physical, mental, and spiritual); and the subdivisions of time—past, present, and future. It is a universal symbol but associated above all with the ancient Celtic culture.

Follow your natural development without force or preconceptions. Let the energy flow according to its own laws. Take care of your physical, mental, and spiritual health at the same time and work for the health of the whole environment of which you are a part.

34

VALKNUT AND THE RUNES
The Search for Divine Knowledge

*Surrender to nature
to learn the truth.*

KEYWORD: WISDOM

The divine speaks a mysterious language: to know it, it is necessary to make a self-sacrifice, abandon the ego, listen, and rely on natural wisdom. In the mythology of the Norse, the ancient ancestors of the Germanic and Scandinavian peoples, the runes are the sacred letters received by the supreme god Odin. Accompanied by Huginn and Muninn, his informant ravens, and his eight-legged steed, Sleipnir, Odin reigns over the world. He hung for nine days from the cosmic tree Yggdrasil and so gained the knowledge of the runes, thus learning the art of divination. The three intertwined triangles are the Valknut (Norwegian for the "knot of the fallen in battle"), symbol of the union of the three worlds (heaven, earth, and hell).

Look around you without expectations. Give up your conceit, abandon yourself, and open your inner eyes: everything will be clear.

35

VEGVÍSIR

The Spiritual Compass

Among the many possibilities, choose a direction and chart your course.

KEYWORD: ORIENTATION

The Spirit is our compass: it never lets us lose our course, even in storms and adverse weather, even if we don't know the direction in which we are traveling. The Vikings' Vegvísir (Icelandic for "wayfinder") is a sacred amulet in Iceland—a signpost, a navigator for journeys through stormy seas and toward safe harbors. It expresses confidence in the divine forces that govern life, the strength of self-confidence even in the toughest trials. By tracing it, carrying it, and contemplating it, we reconstruct our itinerary and reach our destination.

When it feels like all is lost and you see no way out, it's time to tap into your inexhaustible resources. Faith, hope, and courage will ferry you to the shore, beyond the storm.

36

BEAIVI
The Sun Drum of the Sámi

Follow the primal forces of nature to heal and thrive.

KEYWORD: HEALING

Around the sun exist all the creatures of the three worlds—upper, middle, and lower: the living (humans, animals, and vegetables), the stars and stones, the people of the spirits, and the gods. The sun is a feminine divinity, Beaivi; painted in the center of the drum that the shaman uses for healing ceremonies, it is both vehicle and map for his journey in search of the soul of the community, people, and animals. The life of the Sámi, the only remaining native European people (located in northern Scandinavia across Sweden, Finland, Norway, and Russia), revolved around the reindeer and their migrations, which in turn followed the path of the sun, essential for health and survival.

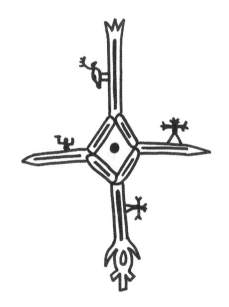

Let the light of the sun guide your path. It shows you the way, allowing you to continue your beautiful journey and overcome any difficulty.

37

KOLOVRAT

The Radiating Sun

Protect your people and life by honoring the principles of coexistence.

KEYWORD: BRIGHTNESS

The movement and radiation of the sun are the source of life. The swastika, a positive and solar sign that has always been present all over the world in many forms, is still venerated in the Indian and Tibetan regions and cultures. It represents light and its uninterrupted circulation. It was perverted by the Nazis, transforming it into an emblem of evil. The eight-ray swastika, or the eight-spoked wheel, is the Kolovrat, a Slavic pre-Christian symbol and the main symbol of the Slavic Native Faith, or Rodnovery. The Kolovrat is sometimes considered to be an attribute of Perun, a Slavic divinity of lightning, appearing on his solar shield with which he protects humanity.

Exchange, circulate, spread life energy for the good of all. Guard your loved ones and nourish them with your light: this is your human fulfillment.

38

SWORD

The Weapon of Virtue

Don't hesitate—make a strong and final decision.

KEYWORD: JUSTICE

Only a pure heart can wield a sword, the chosen weapon of the angel who prevents those who do evil or follow evil from entering paradise. Faith is a warrior, and the sword is discrimination through sacrifice: it cuts and separates evil from good, false from true, vice from virtue. In the Christian world, the sword is a chivalrous symbol of justice, valor, strength, and righteousness and is an extension of the archangel Michael, who defeats the evil dragon of ignorance and impiety to protect all creatures.

Choose the good and defend your truth. If someone is overruling you, face the conflict with the certainty of your reasons until victory.

39

SPIRAL

The Primary Motion

Return with your mind to the origin
of the situation you are experiencing;
evaluate the premises and consequences
of what you are doing.

KEYWORD: EVOLUTION

The essential motions of the cosmos are always the same: expansion and contraction, growth and reduction, opening and closing. Life, like everything else, is born from a point—a seed—and develops in a spiral: from galaxies to shells to the double helix of DNA, all of creation begins from a center and returns to it, crossing it to then re-emerge in the opposite direction, returning to the origin. Indeed, these two movements (expansion and contraction) are simultaneous even if to our perception they appear separate and opposite. Beginning and ending are the same thing. The spiral is one of the most ancient and universal symbols and manifests the union beyond the separations produced by the individual mind: it is the point that becomes a line and returns to the point; it is continuity in change.

What you are experiencing now has presented itself before and will present itself again in the future. To center yourself and expand again, gather your strength and take up the path you already know in a new way.

40
INFINITY
Union with the Whole

Step outside of your
usual boundaries.

KEYWORD: COMPLETENESS

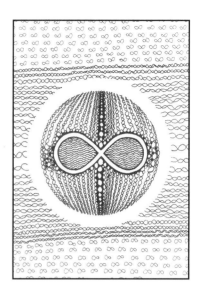

We can understand the world up to a certain point, as far as our senses and knowledge take us: in reality. it is *infinity* that understands *us*. Beyond any separation, beyond the lines we can identify and draw in our limited experience, beyond words and thought, the universe has no boundaries, no beginning, and no end. The graphic symbol unites the dimensions of the known and the unknowable in a double circle: spirit and matter, time and space, human and divine are intertwined and united seamlessly. In mathematics, it is the lemniscate, an eight on its side. On the spiritual plane, it is sublimated matter.

Cultivate the feeling of devotion to the entire universe and its wonderful energy. When you are in the grip of worry, call this immense reality to witness your acts and thoughts.

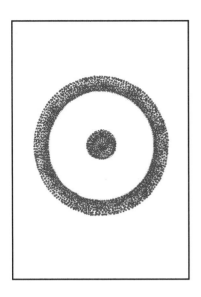

41
DOT AND CIRCLE
The Symbol of Symbols

Everything comes from here; this symbol is the Everything.
All other symbols are elaborations of this one: the essence.
The point is the one, the center that contains all potentiality.
The circle is its extension: it is creation.
The one does not exist without the other.
Concentration and radiation.
Center and circumference.
Being and becoming.
Essence and form.

When you have studied and meditated on all the symbols, leave them, including this one.

You will become a symbol yourself.

Part 3

Sacred Symbols for Coloring, Meditation, and Divination

In the following section, I have included my drawings inspired by each sacred symbol presented in this book. The illustrations are my free artistic interpretation of each symbol. You can use them for your own imaginative and meditative work in several ways:

- You can open the pages of the book at random and meditate on the symbol that appears for you.

- You can use the notes page next to each symbol illustration to write down the reflections, insights, and emotions that the image has evoked for you.

- You can also use the note pages to invent a story, a poem, a song, or any other creation that may come to you.

- You can color the drawings to enter even deeper into the essence of the symbol and unleash your imagination and creativity. To do this, I suggest you reproduce the symbol drawings by photocopying them and coloring these instead, so that you might preserve the book for future use. Once you've colored a symbol illustration, you can hang it up so you might look at it from a distance and

easily meditate on the symbol as if it were a mandala or a painting. Keeping it on display will absorb the surrounding energy and prompt others who see it to share their thoughts with you.

Another way to unleash your creativity and intuition is to do the same work I did when I recreated the original symbols I was researching. You can reproduce the original symbols shown in Part 2 in your own unique interpretation, then color them and use them in your meditation work.

Like all imaginative work, you can also do group drawing and coloring meditations for a fun and enlightening experience. Working with others is a practice that acts as a multiplier of energy that enhances the overall experience for all those involved and allows you to share deeply with one another. So have fun and happy exploring!

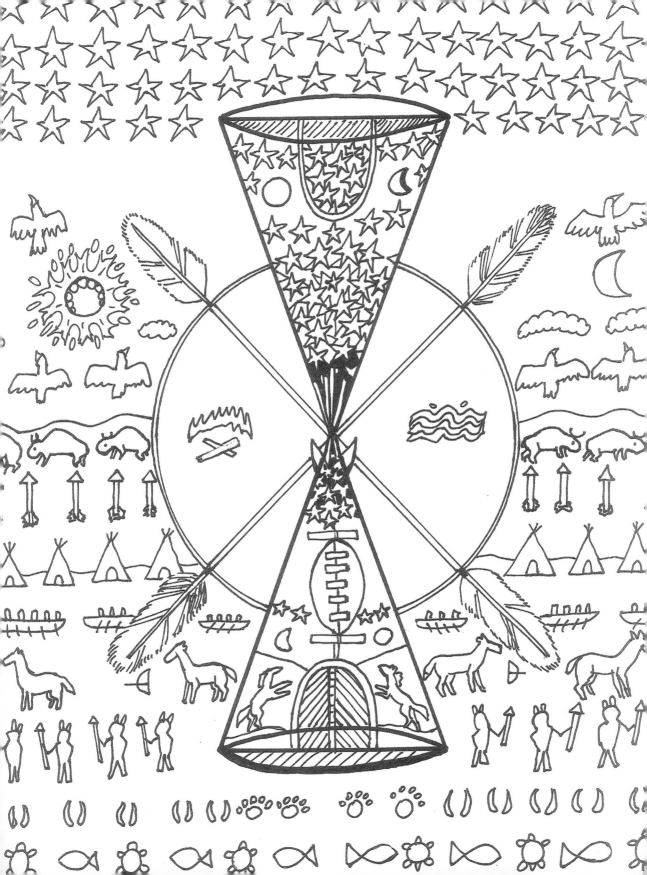

1
KAPEMNI
Notes

2

TOTEM POLE
Notes

3
TZOLK'IN AND HAAB
Notes

4
CHAKANA
Notes

5
MATA KOMOE
Notes

6
TJURUNGA
Notes

7

ENSŌ

Notes

8
TORII
Notes

9
BAGUA
Notes

10
DORJE
Notes

11
DHARMACHAKRA
Notes

12
OM
Notes

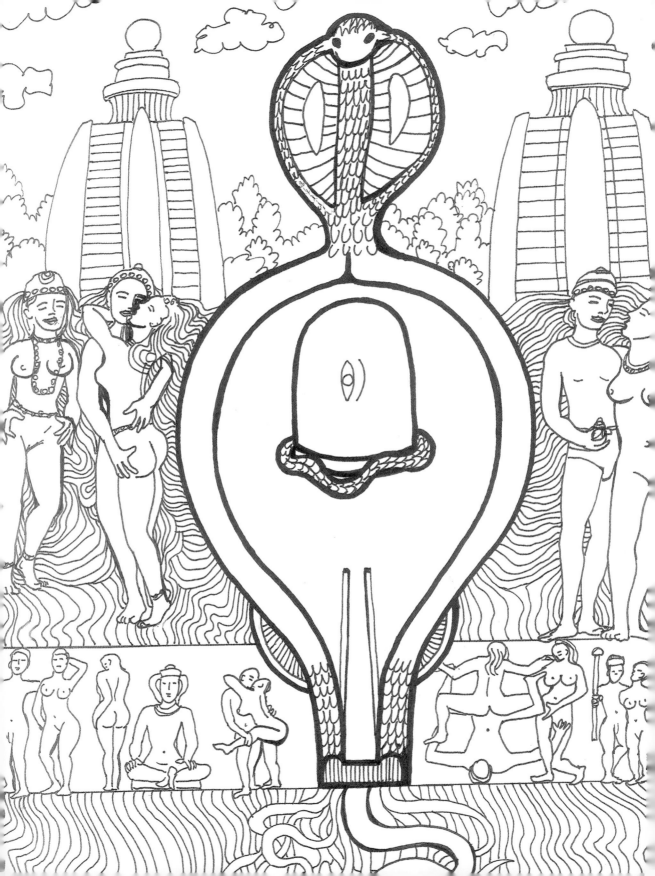

13
LINGAM-YONI
Notes

14
FARAVAHAR
Notes

15
MĀGĒN DĀWĪD
Notes

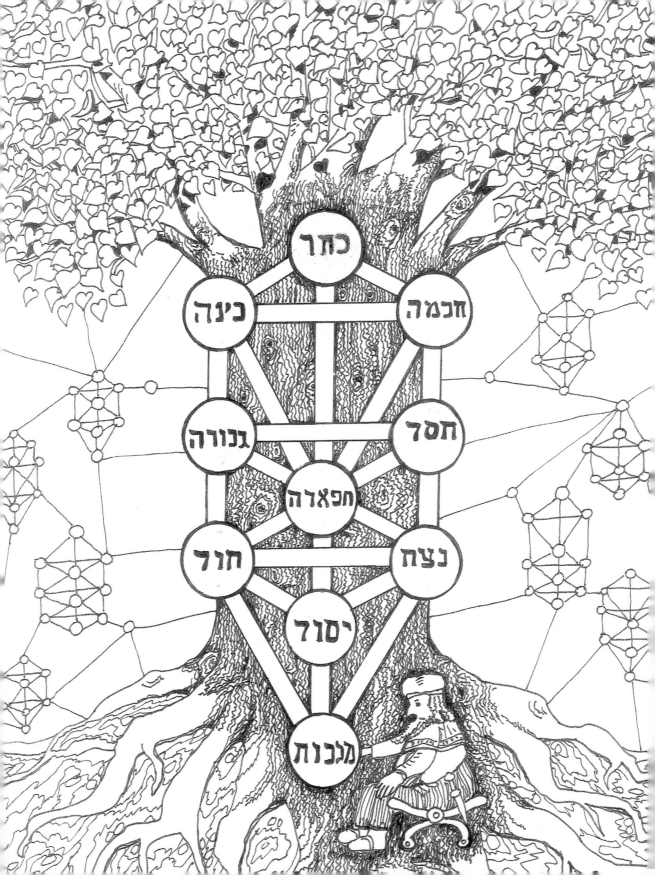

16
ETZ HAYIM
Notes

17
CROSS
Notes

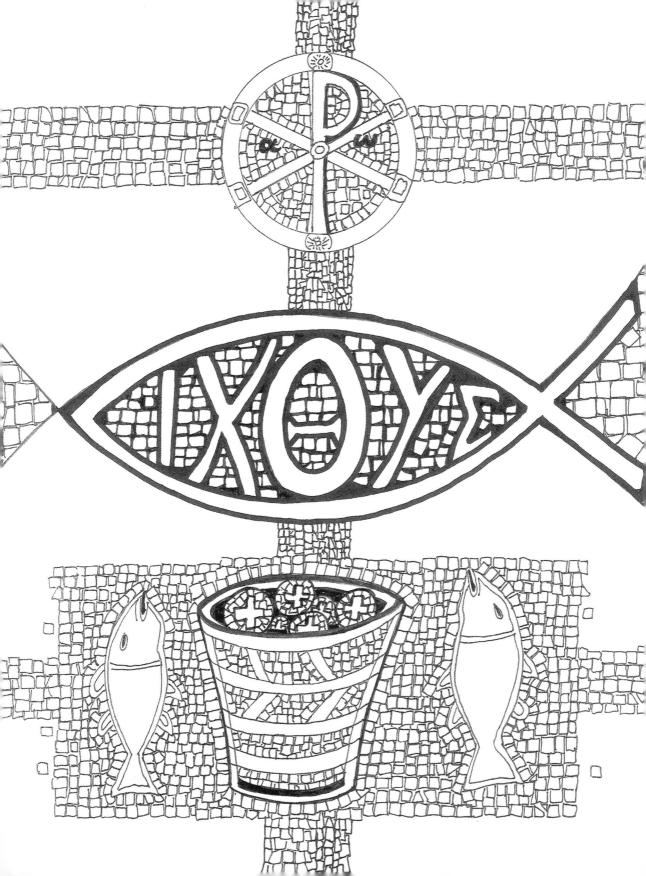

18
ICHTHÝS
Notes

19
CRESCENT MOON
Notes

20
KHAMSA
Notes

21
ANKH
Notes

22
UDJAT
Notes

23
MASK
Notes

24

NYAME YE OHENE
Notes

25
LABYRINTH
Notes

26
LABRYS
Notes

27
CADUCEUS
Notes

28
THE GODDESS
Notes

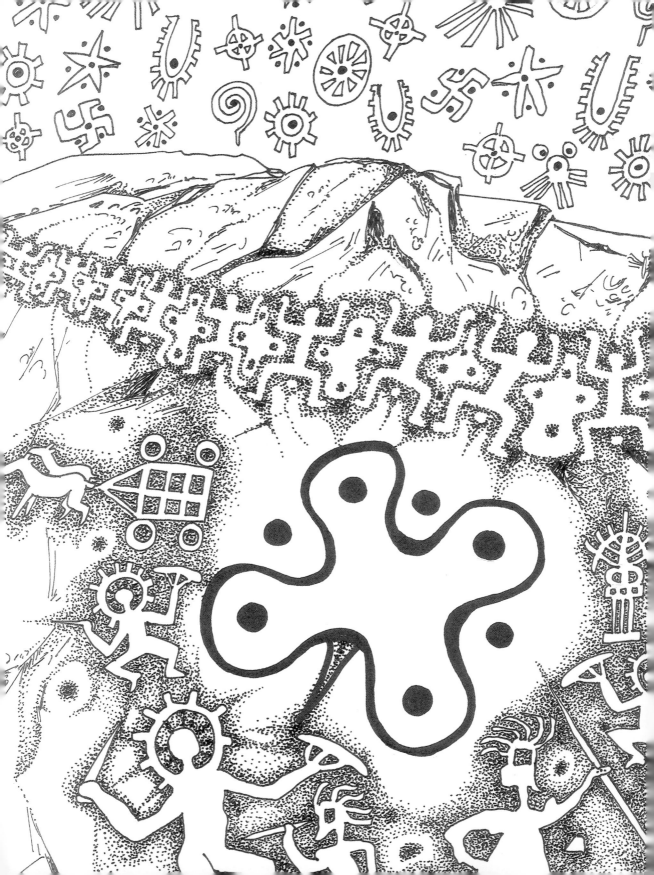

29

CAMUNIAN ROSE

Notes

30
ETRUSCAN LIVER AND MIRROR
Notes

31
OUROBOROS AND THE ALCHEMICAL POT
Notes

32

VITRUVIAN MAN
Notes

33
TRISKELE
Notes

34
VALKNUT AND THE RUNES
Notes

35
VEGVÍSIR
Notes

36
BEAIVI
Notes

37
KOLOVRAT
Notes

38
SWORD
Notes

39
SPIRAL
Notes

40
INFINITY
Notes

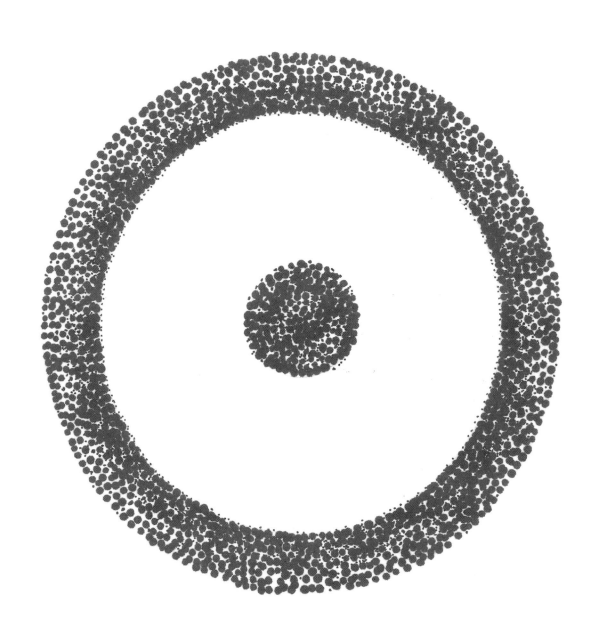

41
DOT AND CIRCLE
Notes

Author's Note

Please note that though I am not an accredited anthropologist, my research and spiritual exploration of these symbols and their meanings was conducted with the utmost respect and sensitivity for the cultures they each belong to. I present in this book and in *The Power of Symbols Deck* my interpretations and passion for the included symbols and invite the reader to approach working with them with respect and an open mind.

Sincerely,
Stefano Fusi

Acknowledgments

I would like to thank the human, animal, vegetable, and natural masters I have met and who have taught me through the stars, the stones, the elements, the encounters, the pages of books, art and music, work, and the events of each day.

I thank my relatives, friends, brothers, loves of the past, present, and future.

I thank Lorenzo Ostuni, master of symbols, who opened the way for me, and the ancient sibyls whose voice he awakened.

About the Author

AUTHOR PHOTO BY ANGELO SCUTERI

Stefano Fusi is an Italian writer, journalist, and painter with a deep commitment to ecology, nature, and health. He has collaborated with leading Italian environmental organizations like World Wildlife Fund and Italia Nostra and has contributed to numerous magazines, including *Qui Touring* and *New Age Music & New Sounds*. Fusi has served as editor in chief of *Il Giornale della Natura* and edited *Anima News*. He has also been a press officer for Red Edizioni and the Interassociation of Arts for Health. Beyond writing, Fusi has led seminars, courses, and events for various organizations. Currently, he works as a ghostwriter, manages a humanitarian fund for the Indigenous Peoples of the Americas, and conducts experiential meetings focused on deep ecology.